GRID DOWN
SURVIVAL GUIDE
SMALL ARMS

PAUL MARKEL

Grid Down Survival Guide
SMALL ARMS

www.whitman.com

© 2015 Whitman Publishing, LLC
3101 Clairmont Road • Suite G • Atlanta, GA 30329

ISBN: 079484264X   EAN: 9780794842642
Printed in the United States of America.

CONTENTS

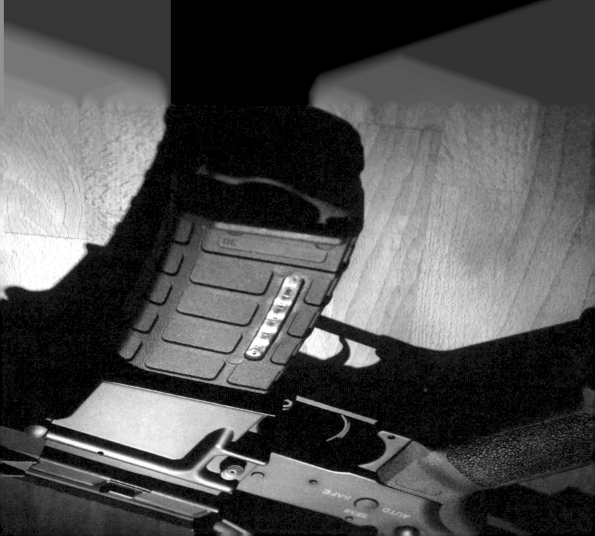

INTRODUCTION

The word "prepper" has become a pejorative term in many circles due to the subject's ever-increasing reputation within popular culture. I find it odd, if not troubling, that as a nation we have devolved into such a state that some members of society find it strange that others wish to ensure that they have adequate food, water, and other staples in their home. When I was a young boy, prepping was the standard for living. Most houses were built with either a fruit cellar or a designated pantry off of the kitchen. It was simply understood that a family would store ample supplies of food in their home. Thus, people stocked food in their pantries, cellars, and various storage areas according to their family's needs. Running out to the grocery store every other day was seen as an impractical waste of time. While I was growing up, my mother would make Saturday morning trips to the grocery store just once every two weeks.

By today's standards, my mother and grandmother would be labeled "preppers." Each spring they planted vegetable gardens, and during the summer and fall, they would can food and put it away for the winter.

Food, water, shelter, clothing, bedding, batteries, fuel supplies, and other essentials were once considered priorities that should be provided by a mother and father. Sadly, far too many of those who inhabit the United States of America see the procuring of their "daily bread" not as a personal responsibility, but as a birth-right to be ensured by a centralized bureaucracy. This mode of thinking promotes the idea that American citizens will never run out of food, water, shelter, or clothing because the government will make certain that every individual will have all of their needs met.

If you have this text in your hands, I feel certain that you do not fall into the category of people who live with this sense of entitlement. You have likely begun to take steps to ensure that your family is prepared and has enough life-sustaining essentials to weather a protracted storm.

INTRODUCTION

Most individuals believe that they are prepared for anything as long as they have procured shelter and stockpiled food, water, and clothing. However, security is just as essential to survival as food and water in the aftermath of a catastrophic event. During an emergency or grid-down scenario, it matters very little how much food, water, supplies, etc., you have stockpiled if no measures have been taken to secure them.

For centuries, the foremost self-defense tool has been the firearm. While they may have changed in their configuration and design, guns remain the most reliable form of self-protection. However, firearms aren't the only weapons that can save your life when the grid goes down. During the next several chapters, we will examine firearms in detail and consider which may be most practical for you, but we will also discuss knives, pepper spray, and tasers and the gear that accompanies them.

INTRODUCTION

SITUATIONAL AWARENESS

I'd be remiss if I didn't highlight situational awareness and avoidance. Situational awareness is a perceptive understanding of your surroundings. It is the ability to cognitively summarize everything taking place around you in a given moment, and from that summary, work out your strategy for reaction. Every person utilizes situational awareness on a daily basis whether they know it or not. Driving is a prime example of the use of situational awareness. In order to be safe on the road you must look ahead, behind, and to your sides regularly to anticipate your course of action. Employing these tactics requires situational awareness.

In a grid-down circumstance, situational awareness should be utilized at every moment. Always be aware of where you are, how to get out if necessary, where a potential attack could take place, and what is available to you in your immediate surroundings that you might be able to utilize to your advantage, etc.

INTRODUCTION

Avoidance complements situational awareness. Think of it like this: every fight you avoid is a fight you win. Situational awareness gives you the ability to know when to avoid a situation or how to combat danger when it cannot be avoided. In the aftermath of a grid-down scenario, the most beneficial and life-preserving tool at your disposal will be your brain. Use it to think tactically and avoid physical confrontation whenever possible. It is often stated that the best prepared individuals are the ones who employ drills based around avoidance and self-defense maneuvers.

Health, strength, and stamina are three important things you can work on and acquire before catastrophe strikes. Strength and stamina often go hand-in-hand with avoidance techniques. You may need to be able to climb, jump, hide, or run long distances in order to avoid or retreat from danger.

INTRODUCTION

On August 29, 2005, the storm surge from Hurricane Katrina caused dozens of breaches in the levee system around New Orleans which led to the flooding of nearly eighty percent of the city. Before Katrina made landfall, Mayor Ray Nagin of New Orleans ordered residents to evacuate. Along with hundreds of thousands of panicked residents, many members of the New Orleans Police Department evacuated with their families.

As soon as Katrina passed, the criminal element emerged and began a violent rampage of looting, robbery, assault, rape, and murder with impunity, as much of the police force had fled with their families prior to the storm. Liquor stores, convenience stores, and drug stores were the initial targets of looters, and many stores were set on fire after their inventories

 REAL WORLD SCENARIO: *HURRICANE KATRINA*

ORIENTAL RUGS
ANTIQUE AND NEW

DONT TRY.
I AM SLEEPING
INSIDE WITH
A BIG DOG,
AN UGLY WOMAN,
TWO SHOTGUNS
AND A CLAW HAMMER

LOOTER
WILL'S

9/4/05
STILL HERE
WOMAN
LEFT FRI.
COOKING
A POT OF
DOG
GUMBO

had been stolen. Once alcohol, tobacco, and drugs had been procured, looters began to secure necessities by ransacking grocery stores.

Residents that chose to stay and protect their homes and businesses were left to fend for themselves. Many of these people, having been raised in the South, were armed. I was part of a massive contingent of law enforcement personnel sent to New Orleans to restore order. A week after the storm passed, we stopped to check on a group of citizens in the Garden District and inquired as to their condition. One man, with a pistol holstered on his hip and a Mossberg 500 shotgun slung over his shoulder, commented, "We're doing all right. I have a generator, my gas grill, and this here (referring to his shotgun) if any of them looters come back around."

 REAL WORLD SCENARIO: *HURRICANE KATRINA*

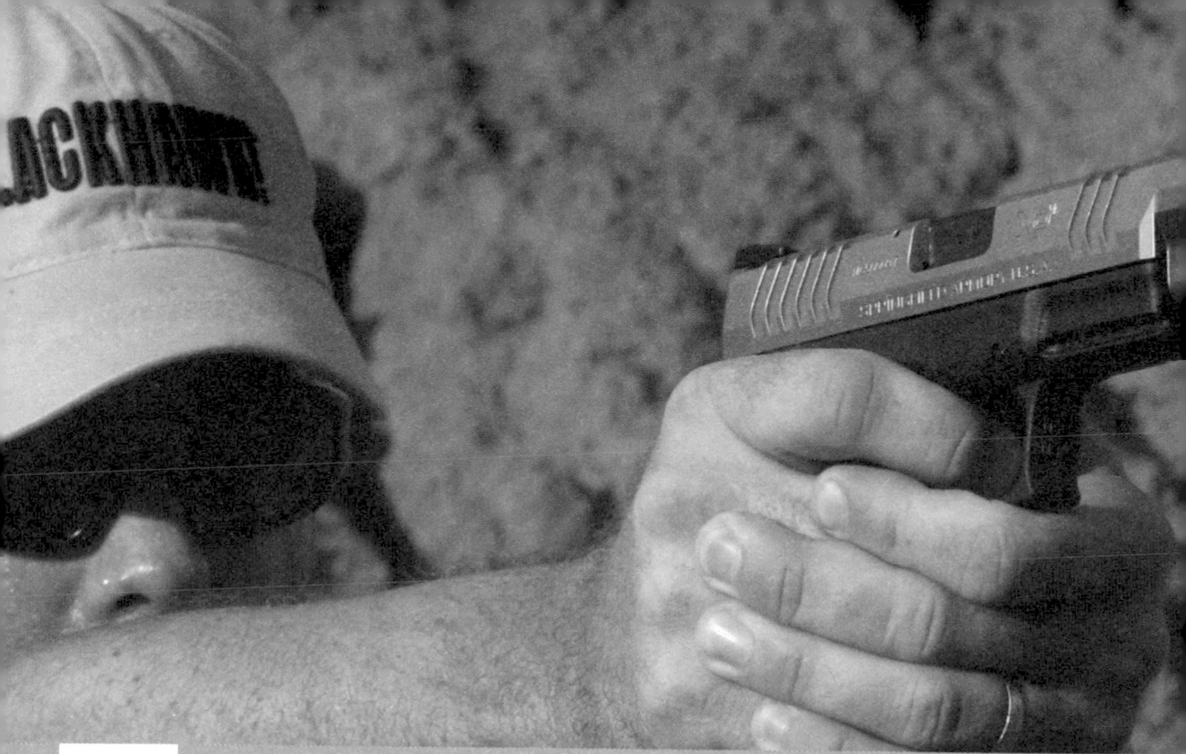

HANDGUNS

The GLOCK 17 is an excellent universal pistol.

Of all the firearms available to the American citizen, the handgun is certainly the one most surrounded by myth and misunderstanding. The reality is that the vast majority of gun owners in the United States spend more time watching handguns being used than using them.

Again, thanks in large part to television and motion pictures, countless citizens have grave misunderstandings about the effectiveness of handguns. Think of your own viewing experiences. In television or movies, handguns never malfunction, and the villains always miss the easy shots. Conversely, the good guys always seem to score spectacular hits with inadequate guns from great distances. I recall the 1970's cop dramas from television. Detectives regularly shot bad guys across long distances with compact handguns like the .38 Special double-action revolver. One bullet fired from hundreds of feet away would send the bad guy tumbling off a rooftop or bridge. The truth is that it doesn't work that way.

The Smith & Wesson M&P9 is a robust, reliable, and ergonomic pistol.

CONVENIENCE VERSUS POWER

People love to toss around the term "stopping power" when it comes to handguns. The reality is that the words "stopping power" and "handgun" do not work well in conjunction with one another. Handguns are unreliable when it comes to stopping power.

 Grid-Down Tip: Flush the term "stopping power" from your vocabulary; it does more harm than good. Many years ago, a grizzled old police sergeant said to me, "If you want stopping power, hit them with your cruiser. That's two thousand pounds of stopping power."

We carry handguns not for their power but for their convenience. A good friend of mine who owns one of the largest private training schools in the United States likes to say, "We carry handguns when there is less than a one percent chance we'll be forced to fight. If the risk is greater, we carry a rifle."

Handguns are popular, in comparison to rifles or shotguns, because they are compact, lightweight, and easy to tote around as we go about our daily lives. Also, most handguns can be concealed in some fashion for discreet protection.

If handguns aren't the all-powerful primary weapons many think they are, then why do we dedicate so much time to the subject? Handguns are important because they are a vital secondary firearm and are integral to your survival during a grid-down situation. Though considered a side-arm (secondary weapon), the handgun is a primary defensive weapon that will serve you well in close, self-defense combat scenarios. You are likely to face such scenarios in cities where much of the crowded population will grow violent in the wake of a catastrophic event.

HANDGUNS

PRACTICAL USE

From a strictly practical standpoint, the handgun is the most difficult of all firearms to use effectively. A handgun is held in either a single-handed grip or a two-handed grip. This standard operating procedure for a handgun is considered a handicap when compared to the added stability provided by the four points of contact needed to operate a rifle or a shotgun. Other detriments of the handgun include a shortened sight radius (distance between rear and front sight) and the relatively heavy trigger pull on most pistols and revolvers.

It takes more time and effort to acquire adequate skills with a handgun than it does with long guns. Handguns are not the simple "point and click" machines you have seen on television or heard about in casual conversation. It is possible to miss your target, even at a close range, with a handgun.

HANDGUNS

There is much to learn when it comes to effectively using a handgun. The two most important areas are the trigger pull and front sight focus. A shooter must be able to focus on the front sight and pull the trigger completely to the rear without disturbing sight alignment on the intended target. This task seems simple when written on paper, but it is very difficult to execute.

THE GOOD NEWS

Currently, the American gun buyer not only has a wider variety from which to choose a handgun than was available just a few years ago, but the quality, economy, and ease of operation of these weapons has improved dramatically in recent years.

Today, a consumer is in jeopardy of becoming rather spoiled in terms of handguns. There are so many high quality firearms at such good

HANDGUNS

The M1911A1 requires dedicated training and practice to master.

prices that some may lose an appreciation for what they have. When I first set out on my journey as an armed citizen and then a professional gun carrier back in the mid-1980's, there were relatively few choices for a centerfire pistol. Most people bought a Colt, a Smith & Wesson, or a Browning Hi-Power. There were others, but they made up only a tiny fraction of available quality duty pistols.

At this point, firearms manufacturers such as Beretta, Colt, Glock, Kahr Arms, Kel-Tec, Ruger, Smith & Wesson, Springfield Armory, etc., have manufactured numerous handguns to meet the needs of most any handgun buyer. Prices can range from very affordable to astronomically expensive.

Also, in addition to the scores of new and innovative weapons flooding the market, many manufacturers are producing a number of excellent accessories. There are innumerable companies producing better sights, holsters, magazines, lasers, and lights than there were just twenty years ago.

HANDGUNS

CHOICES TO MAKE

By the time you read this you will have likely fallen under the influence of a number of different sources that sway your view of handguns. Many people in your life will try to flood your decision-making process with opinions and feelings based on a wide range of personal experiences. Sadly, much of this advice is often outdated or based on faulty information. People will sometimes rely on a random quote from an article about guns they read decades before, instead of doing thorough research.

Purchasing your first handgun for defensive purposes is not an easy process. Your decision is not only clouded by loads of both solicited and unsolicited advice, but options like size, style, caliber, manufacturer, design, color, etc. all factor into the equation. Walking up to the counter in your local gun shop can be a daunting task if it is your first gun purchase.

QUESTIONS

To aid you in your selection, I'd offer a few questions that you should answer for yourself prior to making a purchase for personal protection. Your answer to these questions will determine how large or compact the gun should be. If you are using the gun for home defense or open carry, then it does not need to be compact. Large, full-sized handguns are much easier to shoot and operate than compact or sub-compact guns. For example, a pocket .380 ACP is a ridiculous bedside gun just as a Beretta 92 is going to be extremely challenging to conceal in normal clothing.

Grid-Down Tip: Think about how you will use your firearm. Will you carry it as a primary weapon or as a secondary weapon? Do you want to carry it concealed or open?

HANDGUNS

The Ruger LCR .38 Special revolver is a popular choice for discreet carry as it is compact, lightweight, and easy to use.

Grid-Down Tip: Time for a gut check. How much training, experience, and skill do you possess? How much time are you willing to invest in learning how to use your gun?

Regardless of what you may have heard, a custom 1911 pistol is not a beginner's gun. It's not that you cannot learn to operate the gun; rather, the fact is that, in order to master such a pistol, much practice is needed. Remember the following as a general rule: the more controls or options included in a gun, increases the more time required to master it. Manual safeties, decocking levers, slide releases, and double-action triggers all require training and practice to master.

HANDGUNS

STRIKER-FIRED, 9MM PISTOL

You obviously purchased this book because you are seeking advice on the practicality and utilization of small arms in a post-catastrophe setting. What follows is my advice, based upon three decades of carrying a gun professionally and teaching others to do so.

The polymer-framed, striker-fired pistol chambered in 9mm is my preferred choice for concealed carry, home defense, and open carry. The striker-fired trigger design is easy to manipulate, and it has a built-in redundant safety. These guns also have redundant drop safeties.

With few exceptions, the polymer-framed, striker-fired pistols have few (if any) additional or external controls save for the trigger and magazine release buttons. The slide lock is an administrative feature. Excellent examples of these guns can be found in various Glock pistols, the Smith & Wesson Military & Police Series, and the Springfield Armory

HANDGUNS

XD(M). Kahr Arms makes a pistol called the P9. This gun has probably the best double-action only trigger pull available, and has no superfluous external controls on its slim, ergonomic frame.

The Ruger SR9 deserves honorable mention despite the ridiculous manual safety lever that was installed partially to comply with law enforcement requirements and partially to appease the socialist government of California. All of the aforementioned pistols hold ample 9mm ammunition, have a straight-forward and simple manual of arms, and are affordable.

If I could only have one handgun, it would be a Glock 17. It is infinitely reliable and nearly one hundred percent rustproof. Its magazines are plentiful and inexpensive, and you can easily repair it yourself if necessary.

HANDGUNS

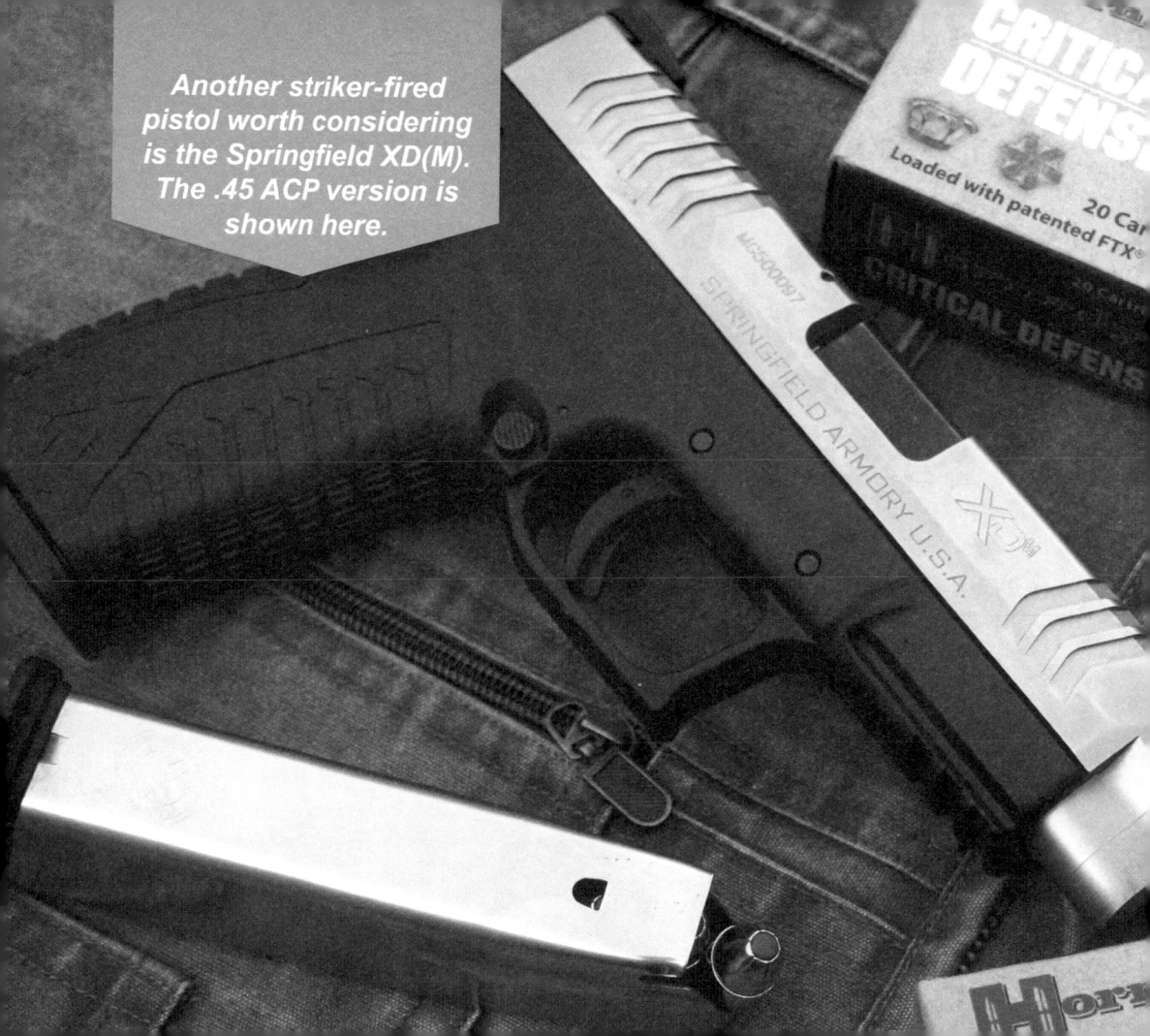

Another striker-fired pistol worth considering is the Springfield XD(M). The .45 ACP version is shown here.

HANDGUN AMMUNITION

When it comes to ammunition for the centerfire handgun, there are two basic categories we will address: practice/target shooting and fighting. Many argue over which type of ammunition is top dog. In the next couple of pages, we will discuss whether or not there is enough of a difference in ammunition to warrant debate.

Regardless of caliber (.38 Special, .380 ACP, 9x19mm, .40 Smith & Wesson, .45 ACP, etc.), there are innumerable differences in designs and offerings for each. For example, I recently checked the Winchester website and found no less than eight different loads for the .45 ACP cartridge.

There are several options when it comes to manufacturers that produce quality ammunition. Federal and Hornady have stellar reputations. Remington and Winchester have been in the ammo business for more than one hundred years and make quality products. Black Hills and CorBon, though they are smaller companies, are favored by many professional gun carriers.

PRACTICE AMMUNITION

Practice or target ammunition is built to be less expensive. Today, there is no such thing as "cheap" ammunition. However, there is ammunition that is more "cost effective." Training or practice ammunition is purposefully built with cheaper components. A manufacturer is able to reduce customer cost when they use less expensive materials. This allows you to shoot more rounds for less money. Practice ammunition will be loaded with a full metal jacket (non-expanding) solid lead bullet, and cases will be standard brass.

One of the cheaper components put into practice or target ammunition is propellant powder. Yes, there are differences in powders, and some are more costly than others. The powder in practice ammunition is generally, though not always, slightly dirtier than the powder used in more expensive ammunition. This means that it tends to give off a gray smoke cloud and leaves behind considerably more carbon on the gun. Practice ammunition also has a tendency to produce a very bright flash.

HANDGUN AMMUNITION

Numerous brands and styles of ammunition are available for the handgun owner. Choose the correct ammo for the anticipated task.

FIGHTING AMMUNITION

When a manufacturer produces a fighting load–one that the shooter will be using to protect his life–premium or more expensive components are used. A quality defensive load will have a controlled expansion bullet. These come in many varieties, but all are designed to expand/open upon striking a target. Expanding bullets have a reduced chance of passing completely through a target, and they will also (potentially) do more damage to a target. Thus, the number of rounds it takes to neutralize a threat will be reduced.

Some of the premium components in self-defense ammunition include nickel cases, sealed (moisture-proof) primers, and flash-reducing propellant powder. Because defensive ammunition is built from premium components, it is naturally more expensive. In this case, you typically get what you pay for. It is expected that fighting ammunition will spend a considerable amount of time loaded in an everyday carry gun.

HANDGUN AMMUNITION

This "stand-by" mode exposes the ammunition to body heat, various climates and weather, and constant shifting or movement, which may degrade ammo. It is my recommendation that you spend a little more money for your defensive ammunition. Money should be no object when it comes to protecting yourself, your loved ones, and your supplies.

CALIBER CHOICES

Despite what you may have been told, when it comes down to hard science, wound ballistics, real-life gunfights, and post-mortem examination, there is hardly a dime's worth of difference between the end result of the 9mm, .40 S&W, and .45 ACP. All of these calibers are completely capable of aiding you in self-defense.

From a physics standpoint, the .40 S&W is a "high pressure" cartridge. The 9mm and .45 ACP are "low pressure" cartridges. Again, all things being equal, the .40 S&W offers considerable recoil in the shooter's hands, and from a mechanical standpoint, it puts more pressure or stress on the handgun.

From a ballistics standpoint, all of the previously mentioned calibers will perform very well when utilizing modern controlled expansion ammunition. If I were forced to choose full metal jacket ammunition, I would pick the .45 ACP, as a 230 grain bullet will travel deep and tear a hole in a target nearly half an inch wide.

In the interest of full disclosure, I was "baptized" nearly thirty years ago as an M1911A1 .45 ACP shooter. I later carried a .40 S&W Glock as a police officer. What do I carry today? I will most likely be found with either a Glock 19 in 9mm or a Kahr P45 in .45 ACP.

HANDGUN AMMUNITION

Reputable companies design premium defensive ammunition to expand, and use more expensive components.

RELIABILITY

Primarily, ammunition must be reliable. Always range test whatever ammo you have decided to load into your gun before you carry it. If the gun cannot go fifty rounds without jamming, you either have a gun that needs to be repaired or you'll need to change ammunition.

Even with premium, fighting ammunition I would encourage you to buy an extra box and run at least twenty-five to fifty rounds of that load through your gun the first time out. Most modern firearms will feed any type of ammunition, but that's not a guarantee. Test it before you bet your life on it.

HANDGUN AMMUNITION

SHOTGUNS

Remington 870 with stock, finish, and sight upgrade from Wilson Combat.

Recommending that a well-prepared citizen own a shotgun is really a "no-brainer." In a grid-down situation, a shotgun will be a very versatile weapon in your arsenal. The shotgun is not only a great gun for self-defense, but it is also a great all-around hunting tool as it can fire various loads that can kill anything from small critters and water fowl to large woodland game. The most important questions to address are what kind of shotgun should you purchase, and what gauge should you choose?

An interesting bit of shotgun knowledge that you might not be aware of is the origin of the word "gauge" as opposed to "caliber." The gauge of a shotgun is named for the number of lead balls it takes to constitute a pound of weight in that specific bore diameter. For example, it would take 12 round lead balls of a specific bore diameter to add up to a pound—filling up a 12 gauge shotgun. The only exception to this rule is the .410 shotgun. That ammunition is measured by caliber (inches) not gauge.

SHOTGUNS

The 12 and 20 gauges are the bestselling gauges in the United States. Yes, 10, 16, and 28 gauge fowling pieces are available, but their ammunition tends to be more expensive and harder to find. The .410 bore shotguns are easy to find, but the ammunition tends to be more costly than the large diameter shotgun shells.

ACTION

When it comes to shotguns, you have hinge-action (break-open) in single and double-barreled configurations. There are also pump/slide action, and semi-automatic (gas-operated) shotguns. Occasionally you can still find a lever-action shotgun.

If your budget is very tight ($100 or less) a single-shot hinge-action gun is likely your best choice. A less limited budget (in the $200 to $400 range) will get you a quality pump-action shotgun from Mossberg, Maverick, Remington, and possibly a Benelli Nova if they happen to be on sale.

SHOTGUNS

Semi-automatic shotguns, such as those from Benelli, Beretta, Mossberg, or Remington, are attractive weapons. The price of a gas-operated shotgun will be considerably higher than a traditional pump-action model. Also, depending on the model, these shotguns may be finicky eaters. In my experience, I've found that the Benelli Super Black Eagle II will consume anything from light bird shot to heavy weight duck and goose loads. Conversely, many gas-operated guns will cycle only high brass, hard-kicking ammunition.

Specialty shotguns, such as the Saiga-12 semi-automatic or the Kel-Tec KSG 12, are considerably more difficult to find in the marketplace. The KSG holds 15 rounds of standard 12 gauge ammo in a gun that is shorter than a standard Remington 870. In contrast, the Saiga-12 is fed with detachable box magazines. The price tags on both guns might give you sticker shock, as they run approximately $700 - $1,000.

PRACTICALITY

Depending on your level of experience, you may already have a favorite gauge of shotgun. If you are a relative neophyte, my recommendation would be the 12 gauge. There is simply far more ammunition available for that gauge. Your tastes and confidence level may differ from mine, and that is quite all right. In the end, the choice is yours to make based upon your preferences.

If I were to be limited to the purchase of only one shotgun, I would choose a 12 gauge pump-action model. In my mind, the Mossberg 500/590 and the Remington 870 are both quality 12 gauge shotguns. Each of these models has different features, but they perform on an equally excellent level. The Benelli Nova and Weatherby 459 both deserve honorable mention.

A pump-action 12 gauge is easily the king of versatility. Being manually operated, there is little concern of whether or not the gun

SHOTGUNS

The classic Remington 870 pump-action 12 gauge shotgun with traditional wooden stock and blue steel configuration.

will cycle with low or high brass shells. Most all modern pump-action 12 gauge shotguns will chamber shells up to 3 inches in length. This allows the shooter to kill snakes with trap load or bears with slugs (and everything else in between).

REALITY CHECK

A shotgun is an excellent utility tool and capable of performing tasks a rifle or pistol would be hard pressed to accomplish. However, the shotgun is not "magical." Some people believe that all you have to do when faced with a threat is pump the action on your shotgun and your potential attacker will scurry away in fear. First of all, that advice assumes that your threat will actually hear the sound and recognize what it is. Any person who breaks into your house or stronghold is not likely an individual with a healthy respect for the sound of a Remington 870.

Any defensive strategy that is predicated upon the cooperation of the attacker is inherently flawed and should not be relied upon for self-

SHOTGUNS

preservation. This goes for "racking" or pumping the action on shotguns, pointing unloaded guns, and trying to scare bad guys with red laser dots from laser sights or blue sparks from a stun gun. It is actually illegal, in most areas, to fire warning shots to ward off potential attackers. Some aggressors will surrender or flee at the sight of a gun. In fact, many will. However, you should not build your defensive strategy based upon the assumption that a dangerous individual will be sufficiently impressed by sights or sounds to stop their threatening behavior. You should never point your gun at anyone to scare them. If you are faced with a lethal threat, it is imperative that you be mentally prepared to take the steps necessary to stop that threat. This includes taking a kill shot.

Grid-Down Tip: This principal is infinitely important in a grid-down scenario as people will become desperate and will do the unthinkable to sustain their own lives. Normal methods of intimidation will likely not be effective in a post-disaster environment because desperate people will do what they must to survive if civilization crumbles. Even good people are capable of horrible things when the grid goes down.

SHOTGUNS

00 BUCKSHOT MYTH-BUSTING

One of the most misunderstood types of ammunition is the 12 gauge 00 buckshot shell. Think of your shotgun as if it were a sledgehammer. Generally, a single 00 buckshot shell will deliver eight or nine .33 caliber pellets on target with the single press of the trigger. That is a lot of heavy, fast-moving lead being delivered on target.

The popular misunderstanding and favored gun shop advice is that it is impossible to miss with a shotgun. This misconception often dominates conversations at public ranges and online forums. Indeed, you can miss with a shotgun. Ask any trap or skeet shooter. Ask a dove or duck hunter. It is possible to miss.

Consider this: depending on the load in question, 00 buckshot patterns will spread an average of one-half to one inch per yard when fired from a cylinder bore shotgun with no added choke. If we go with the FBI 21 foot rule (which states that if an attacker with a knife is less than

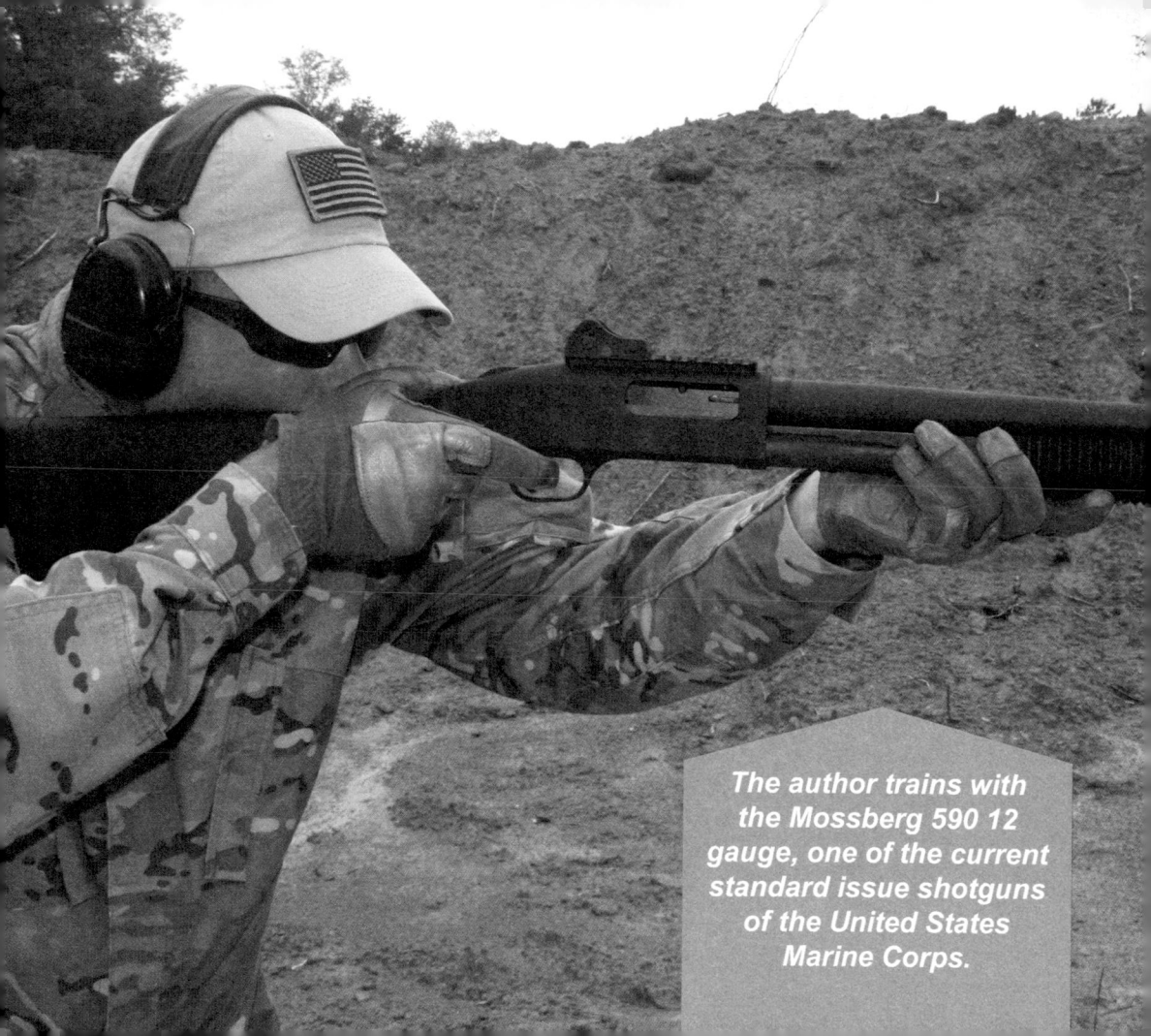

The author trains with the Mossberg 590 12 gauge, one of the current standard issue shotguns of the United States Marine Corps.

21 feet away, you will not have time to draw your gun and fire before being stabbed) your 00 buck pattern will be somewhere between 3.5 and 7 inches across at that distance.

If you are talking about using a shotgun for home or camp defense, a seven yard shot is a long shot. Even if you stretch it to ten yards, the pattern is still tight enough that you could completely miss a man-sized target if you decide to just "point" the gun in the general direction and fire. If you must use a shotgun to save your life, you should shoulder the gun, look down the bore, find a front sight of some sort, and then pull the trigger. Hollywood hip shooting is a bad joke played upon an ignorant public.

SHOTGUNS

SHOTGUN AMMUNITION

Federal's "Flight Control" 00 buckshot patterned at various distances.

All shotgun ammunition falls into three basic categories: low brass, high brass, and single projectile. There are also certain specialty loads that I will touch on later.

LOW BRASS

The term "low brass" refers to a case head that is short or "low." Low brass shells are relatively light recoiling as they have a smaller, lighter powder charge than their cousins. Low brass loads, regardless of the manufacturer, are utilitarian and can be used to kill birds, snakes, small game, etc.

Some would offer that birdshot is ideal for home defense as you will only be taking shots at close range. I would disagree for two reasons. First, in a life or death situation, you will want the most from your shotgun. Birdshot is not the best option for protecting yourself. Secondly, loading a firearm under the assumption that you will only be taking a close range shot is a foolish gamble.

Yes, at close range, birdshot will create a horrible wound. However, I would like to remind you that the purpose of lawful defense against a deadly threat is to completely stop an attacker as fast as physiologically possible, not to inflict painful wounds.

HIGH BRASS

The "high brass" shot shell will have a heavier powder charge designed to drive the payload harder and farther. Goose, duck, and turkey loads are most often high brass and hard-kicking on the shoulder. Traditional buckshot loads for hunting are also heavy thumpers on both ends.

Understanding that so much recoil was not necessary, many of the big ammunition companies have released "tactical" or "self-defense" buckshot loads that deliver 8 pellets of 00 buck with less pounding on the shoulder of a shooter.

SHOTGUN AMMUNITION

Tactical buckshot has been put to good use by American law enforcement officers and armed citizens alike. Federal Cartridge offers a load that patterns tightly and uses the company's patented "flight control" wad. The load is a dream to shoot in a fighting shotgun.

In addition to 00 buckshot, you can purchase 0 buck, 000 buck, #1, #4, and BB loads, just to name a few. Regardless of the load you choose for fighting, you should take the time to pattern it on cardboard at various distances. Often, magazine ads don't mirror reality, and your gun may not pattern as well as the test gun used at the ammunition factory.

SINGLE PROJECTILE

Opinions vary greatly when it comes to firing a single projectile from a shotgun. Some people view the shotgun slug as ammunition that allows a shotgun to mimic a rifle. In a sense, this view is correct. Slugs can also make the shotgun a more precise firearm if the gun has some type of sighting system on it.

As with buckshot, slug ammunition is much further ahead of what was available to your grandfather. You can choose from the standard solid lead "Foster" slug, copper-plated slugs wrapped with a plastic sabot, or compressed copper "frangible" slugs that travel as a single, solid piece and then come apart rapidly when they strike a solid target.

Recently, Winchester introduced a product called the "segmented slug." It is a single Foster-style slug that is pre-scored in a press before it is loaded into the shell. The result is a one-ounce lead slug that remains intact as it flies through the air. When the segmented slug hits something solid, it breaks into three equal parts. I first saw this load demonstrated on ballistic gelatin. Then I took it to the field where I used it to kill a wild hog. If I were shopping for slugs, the PDX1 Segmented Slug from Winchester would be high on my list.

SHOTGUN AMMUNITION

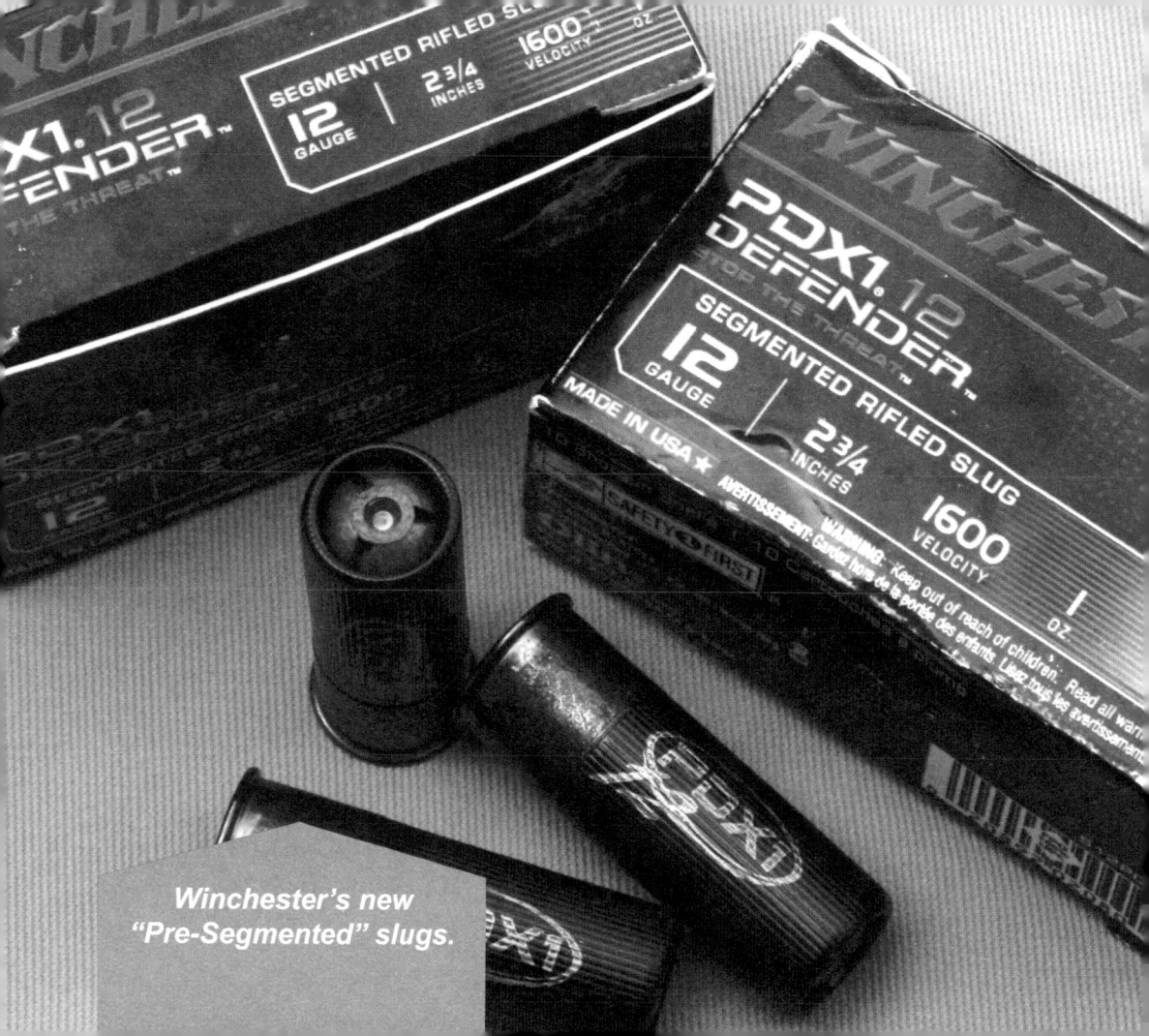

Winchester's new "Pre-Segmented" slugs.

SPECIALTY LOADS

Numerous unique or specialty loads exist for the 12 gauge shotgun. Most of them were designed and developed for law enforcement to use for riot control. Beanbag rounds, rubber buckshot, rubber slugs, tear gas or OC cartridges, flechette rounds, buck and ball combinations, etc., all are attractive alternatives to defensive ammunition.

When it comes to using some type of less-than-lethal shotgun shell, I would offer a word of caution. A shotgun is a firearm. Just because you load it with rubber buckshot does not mean that you can treat a shotgun as anything other than a shotgun.

Far too many citizens think that the answer to their home defense situation is to load a shotgun with non-lethal rubber shot ammunition. Some of these people then view their shotgun as on par with a can of mace. However, these specialty loads can be lethal projectiles. Rubber shotgun ammunition was designed for police forces and prison guards to use during riots and is not meant to be utilized for home defense.

In order to remain within the confines of the law, a citizen may only shoot a firearm at another human being if they are in fear for their life or in fear of serious bodily harm. If you discharge a firearm with intent to hit a human target, then you are exercising deadly force regardless of the ammo you use. Why would you deliberately use less-than-lethal weaponry in a scenario that calls for deadly force?

If you are confronted with one or more violent marauders bent on your destruction, then your goal should be to stop them as fast and effectively as possible. Trying to be "nice" or "civil" may cost you your life. There is no room for "nice" in mortal combat.

SHOTGUN AMMUNITION

L.A. RIOTS, MAY 1992

On May 29, 1992, racial tensions in the city of Los Angeles reached a boiling point in response to the acquittal of four Los Angeles Police officers accused of beating a suspected criminal, Rodney King. Many in the city of Los Angeles and surrounding communities took to the streets and started a weeklong rebellion of theft, robbery, assault, and murder. All told, more than sixty murders are credited to the lawlessness, as well as millions of dollars in property damage and theft.

A great example of self-defense during the riots is that of the prepared citizens defending their homes and businesses in what was known as "Korea Town." Numerous business owners and their families, having taken the time to arm themselves long before the violence began, stood

 REAL WORLD SCENARIO: L.A. RIOTS

up against the waves of people taking advantage of the chaos to loot, rob, rape, and murder.

When faced with such armed resistance, the criminals fled and choose weaker, unprotected targets. The LAPD and Los Angeles County Sheriff's deputies were too overwhelmed to protect individual homes and businesses. These riots were so chaotic that it took military intervention to end them. It should be noted that, when the riots began, Los Angeles declared a state of emergency and forbade gun and ammunition sales.

⊕ REAL WORLD SCENARIO: *L.A. RIOTS*

RIFLES

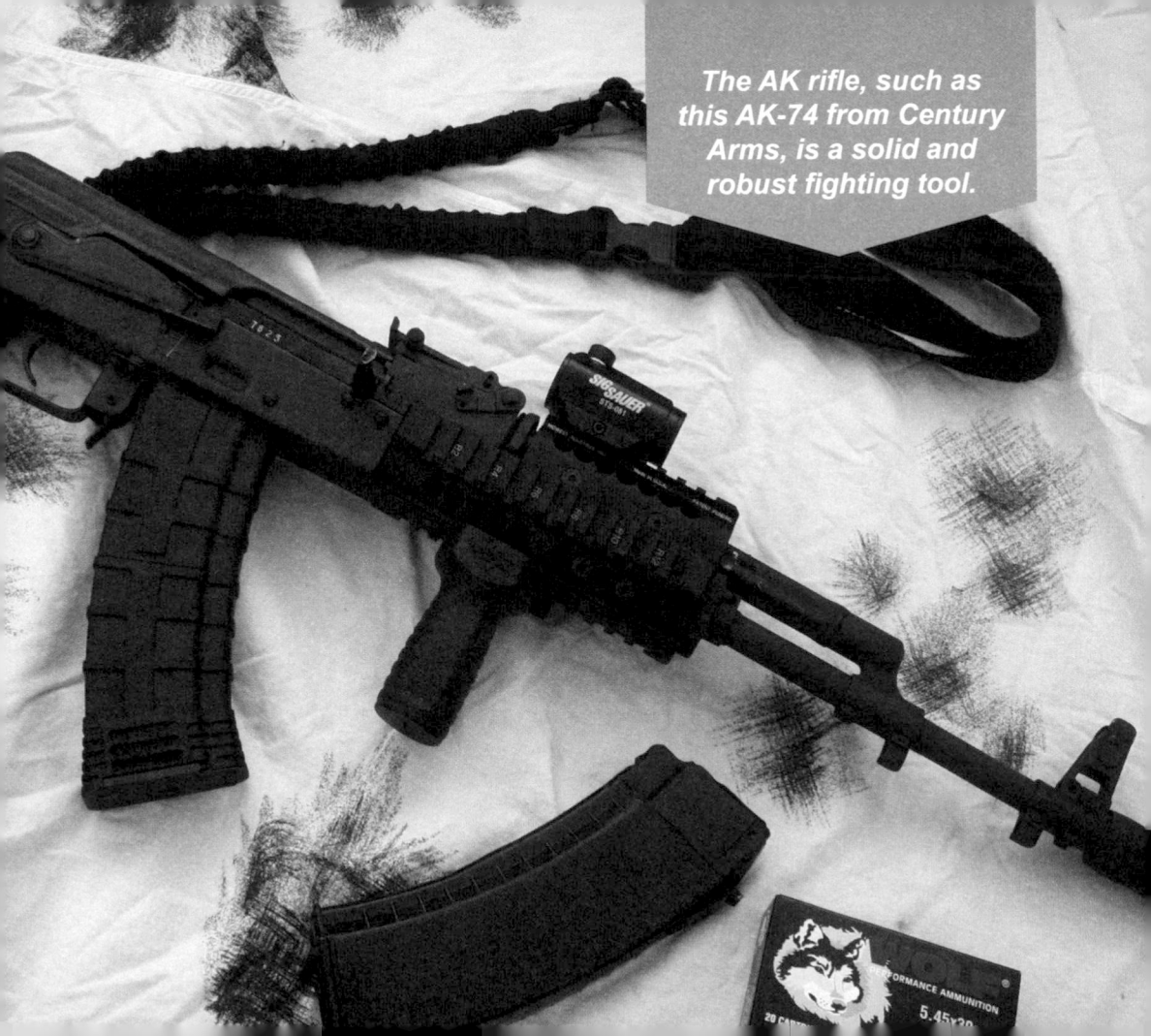

The AK rifle, such as this AK-74 from Century Arms, is a solid and robust fighting tool.

The rifle remains one of the most effective tools in the well-prepared citizen's firearm arsenal. From close range room clearing to long range sniper shots, the rifle provides a wide range of utility in multiple environments. Rifles equip the modern shooter with a force multiplier as an offensive or defensive weapon. In a grid-down scenario, you may need to utilize your rifle as an offensive weapon in certain situations. For example, you might need to take back precious supplies that have been stolen from you by marauders. Rifles are also very effective hunting tools.

Our discussion of rifles is going to diverge into two primary purposes: utility and personal defense. Subcategories will include action and caliber/chambering. As with the handgun or shotgun considerations, choosing a rifle can be a daunting task because there are so many from which to choose.

Many Americans consider the rifle a tool only to be used for targets at a great distance. While it is true that rifles are distance weapons, you should also consider centerfire rifles to be powerful tools when addressing any threat.

UTILITY

For basic utility, a .22 LR rifle is a tough option to beat. Despite the fact that .22 LR ammunition has been hard to find lately, it remains one of the most prevalent and popular rifles in United States, if not the world.

Killing varmints and pest animals as well as harvesting small to medium-sized game are all tasks that you can handle with a .22 LR rifle, the right ammo, and a steady hand. The .22 LR rifle is an excellent all around tool because it is easy for any member of the family to use. Even teenagers and adolescents should have little trouble handing a .22 rifle.

The .22 rifle barely moves when a cartridge is discharged and most are lightweight and easy to manipulate. These guns are also relatively quiet in standard configuration and extremely quiet when combined with a suppressor. (Note: Even with a suppressor, super-sonic ammunition will still "crack.")

RIFLES

An AR rifle chambered in .22 LR is a great tool for practice and small game chores.

Of the various styles of AR, the mid-length gas system is the author's preferred design.

SELF-PROTECTION

When it's time to fight with a rifle in your hands, a .22 LR should be your last choice. There are two primary and important reasons for this. First, .22 LR ammunition is relatively feeble when it comes to incapacitating large animals. Secondly, manufacturers build rimfire ammunition, like .22 LR, to be inexpensive, and it will never function as reliably as modern centerfire ammunition.

For these reasons, we base our discussion of fighting/personal defense rifles around modern centerfire cartridges. I'd take a .22 over no gun at all, but with so many quality arms in existence, there are many better alternatives.

ACTION

The semi-automatic, gas-operated rifle is the most popular offering available today, but many others are on the market such as bolt or lever-action guns. Like the shotgun, some semi-automatic guns can be finicky eaters.

The decision of which action you purchase should be based upon your experience, what you expect to use the gun for, and your disposable income. As a well-prepared citizen, you should primarily base your purchase of a rifle on reliability, parts that are readily available, and fire superiority. When fending off a band of marauders, you don't want to bring a lever-gun to a semi-auto fight. However, don't forget that other guns can also be used to trade for needed items in a grid-down scenario.

If you survive the initial collapse of a grid-down scenario, you will most likely settle at a retreat location or defensive position. Whether in an urban or open-country environment, you may have to engage a target at various distances. You may need an assortment of rifles for multiple distances.

 **RIFLES**

LEVER-ACTIONS

Lever-action rifles, particularly of the .30-30 variety, are easy to come by, and you'll find them on sale at your local sporting goods store (every year during hunting season). The Marlin 336 lever-action rifle chambered in the .30-30 Winchester load typically sells in the $500 range.

Lever-action carbines chambered in pistol caliber cartridges, while easier to shoot than handguns, pale in comparison to a genuine rifle. Those skilled in their use can cycle the action on a lever rifle quite fast. It simply takes training and practice.

BOLT-ACTIONS

As for bolt-action rifles, Ruger, Savage, and Mossberg produce quality bolt-guns in the $400 to $500 range with their economy models. All the aforementioned rifles chamber serious ammunition, such as the .308 Winchester and .30-06 Springfield.

RIFLES

In the military surplus market, the most prevalent and least expensive rifles are those built on the Mosin-Nagant action. The Mosin-Nagant Model 1891/30, commonly referred to as the 91/30, is a robust, reliable, and time-proven design. They are ridiculously inexpensive when you consider that they fire the 7.62x54R (rimmed) cartridge, which is extremely powerful and is essentially the Russian equivalent of our .30-06 Springfield.

The full-sized 91/30 rifles are just over four feet long and nearly six feet when the eighteen inch bayonet is attached. Numerous carbine length versions of this rifle exist, with the Russian M44 and Chinese Type 53 being the most common.

Prices for surplus Mosin-Nagant rifles range from $100 to $200 generally, although the recent gun craze and weakening of the U.S. dollar have seen prices rise. Using the median price of $150 you could legitimately equip four adults with rifles for only $600. Also worth considering, ammunition for these rifles is still plentiful, and as far as centerfire .30 caliber rifle ammunition is concerned, it is attractively priced.

RIFLES

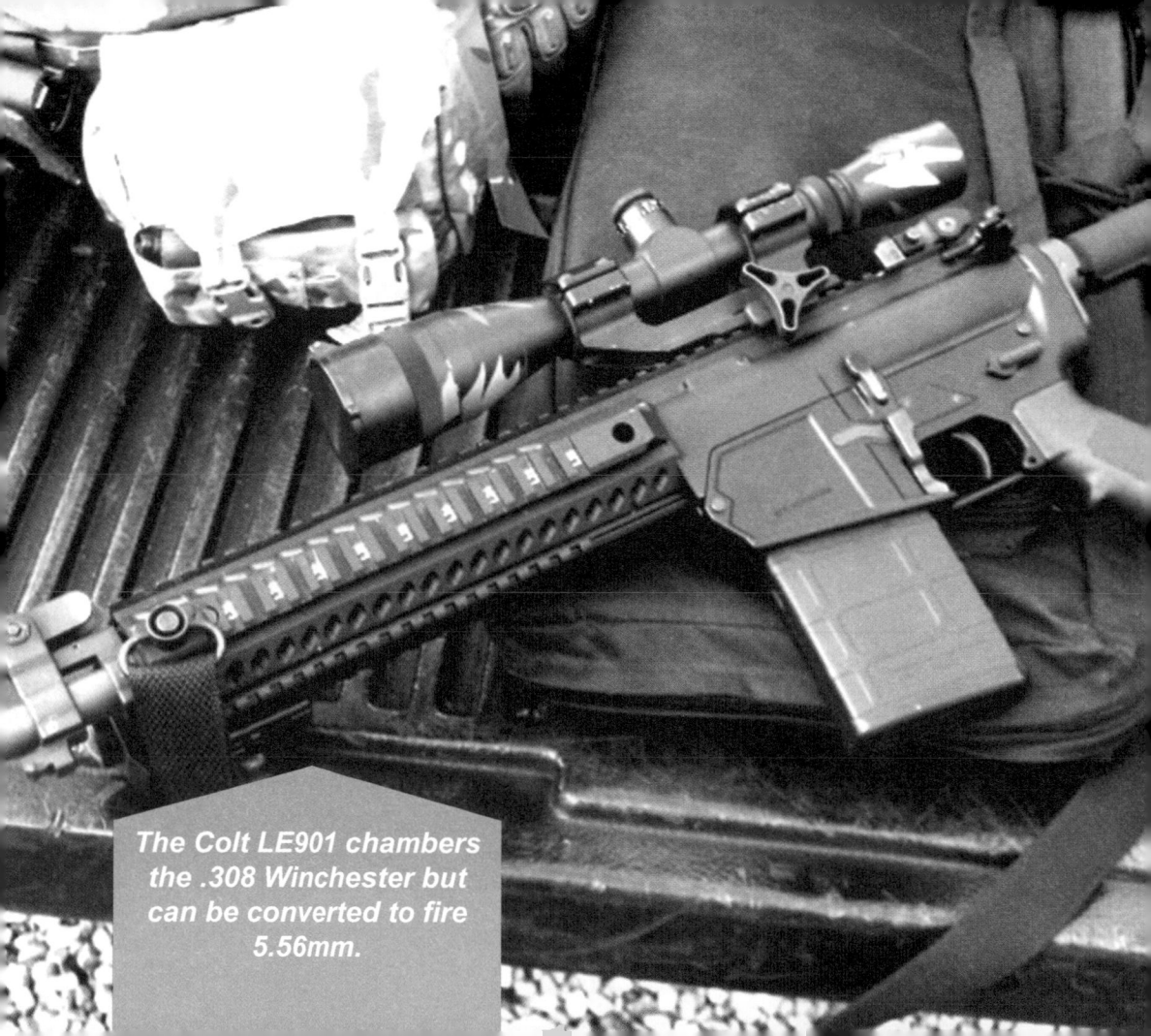

The Colt LE901 chambers the .308 Winchester but can be converted to fire 5.56mm.

The author killed this 200 plus pound boar with a Wilson Combat 6.8 SPC rifle.

Many individuals are currently seeking higher quality bolt-guns. A quality bolt-action rifle in the right hands can give a strategic edge for long range defense or hunting. For the bolt-guns, the .308 remains the most commonly purchased caliber in the prepper market. It is widely available, relatively inexpensive, and incredibly accurate up to 1,000 yards or more. However, the major drawback to a bolt-action rifle is the fact that you can only shoot one round at a time. You must also have quality optics to maximize your accuracy. Never skimp on the glass. Modern quality optics have either a bullet drop compensator and/or a first focal plane type of reticle. High quality optics are another force multiplier when you are in survival mode.

THE KING OF MODERN RIFLES

In modern America, there are two types of rifles vying for the top spot. As much as I love my Kalashnikov (AK) rifles, the AR-15 is my number one choice. Put quite plainly, rifles built upon Eugene Stoner's original Armalite Rifle Model 15 design are the most prevalent in the U.S.A.

The modern black rifle, AR-15, M4, or the Modern Sporting Rifle (whatever name you like to call it) is not only the most prolific design, but it is also the most versatile and has more parts and accessories available than any other. This is particularly important for the well-prepared individual. Firearms are simple machines, and machines sometimes break down and need parts replaced.

AR-rifles are the most versatile firearm available. Models with flattop upper receivers can be outfitted with iron sights, red dot 1:1 optics, or magnified riflescopes. By simply pushing out two pins, the end user can swap upper receivers and change their rifle from a .223 Remington to a 6.8SPC II, a .300 AAC Blackout, or even the varmint killing .204 Ruger, among others. This type of rifle can also be broken down quickly in the field for cleaning with no tools necessary. Note: As a well-prepared individual, you need to understand that battery-powered optics will eventually fail, and glass optics can break. It is imperative to have iron sights as a back-up on all weapons.

RIFLES

Because the lower receiver is technically the "firearm" from a legal standpoint, you can purchase AR-15 upper receivers online or over the counter. By purchasing a single lower receiver, you can assemble a lightweight home defense carbine one day and swap it for a full length rifle barrel with magnified optic to kill coyotes the next day. However, in certain scenarios, multiple complete rifles may benefit a prepper more than a rifle built with multiple, interchangeable parts.

AR-15 style rifles are available in the aforementioned .204 Ruger, .223 Remington, 5.56x45mm NATO, 6.8 SPC II, 7.62x40 Wilson Tactical, .300 AAC Blackout, .264 Les Baer Custom AR, 6.5 Grendel, 458 SOCOM, and the monster .50 Beowulf. Many other chamberings exist as well, making for a host of caliber choices from a single platform, not to mention the possibility of .22 LR upper conversions for inexpensive training and practice.

A FAMILY RIFLE

One feature that makes the modern AR-15 such an attractive option for the prepared individual or family is the fact that almost any physically fit adult or teenager should be able to operate the rifle. In the M4 configuration, the stock adjusts to fit people of all shapes and sizes.

The gas-operated action combined with the buffer/buffer spring recoil system allow for very mild recoil as far as centerfire rifles are concerned. Teenagers routinely compete and hunt with modern AR-15 rifles and with great success.

From a personal standpoint, my wife, teenage daughter, and son all enjoy shooting my AR-style rifles. The fact that they are semi-automatic and hold ample ammunition for a self-protection scenario makes them excellent home defense tools. A mother protecting her children with an AR-15 rifle is a formidable opponent, even for multiple home invaders.

RIFLES

Inexpensive and powerful, the Mosin-Nagant rifle (Century Arms) is a great choice for a tight budget.

TRAINING, PRACTICE, CONFIDENCE

Regardless of your action or caliber choice, training and practice are the keys to confidence and success. While the modern AR is versatile and user friendly, it is much different than most other traditional rifles you may have grown up shooting.

Do not wait until the grid goes down to start training or sighting-in your weapons. If you've never had any formal training with an AR, it is definitely in your best interest to seek out professional instruction from a qualified teacher. You will learn more about proper technique and shooting skills in a two-day course than you will in a year on your own.

Whether you live in an arid environment or a swampy wetland, your gear and weapons need to function in that environment. Many modern rifle manufacturers use specialty coatings that provide added protection from the elements. It is imperative that you know how to break down your rifle so you can properly clean and oil the parts. Always keep a

RIFLES

spare parts kit handy and have everyone in your group do the same. Having the same weapons system or weapons with interchangeable parts in your group or family dramatically increases your chance for survival. This becomes invaluable when one group member is in the position of having to pick up and use another member's weapon. With weapon uniformity, each group member will know how to use any gun in the group arsenal as if it were his own.

RIFLE AMMUNITION

Ammunition and firearms prices have, within the last few years, fluctuated dramatically as the political climate surrounding civilian firearm ownership has grown increasingly volatile. These circumstances should not deter individuals from purchasing firearms and ammunition. In fact, as the political machine makes every effort to erode your gun rights, you should make an extra effort to procure what your budget allows in terms of firearms. You will not regret taking this action if a catastrophic event occurs and the grid goes down. A truly prepared individual understands that when disaster strikes, stores won't be open and their inventories will be depleted due to looting. You should stock plenty of ammunition so that you're prepared should a grid-down scenario occur. Naturally, the same goes for food, batteries, and other supplies.

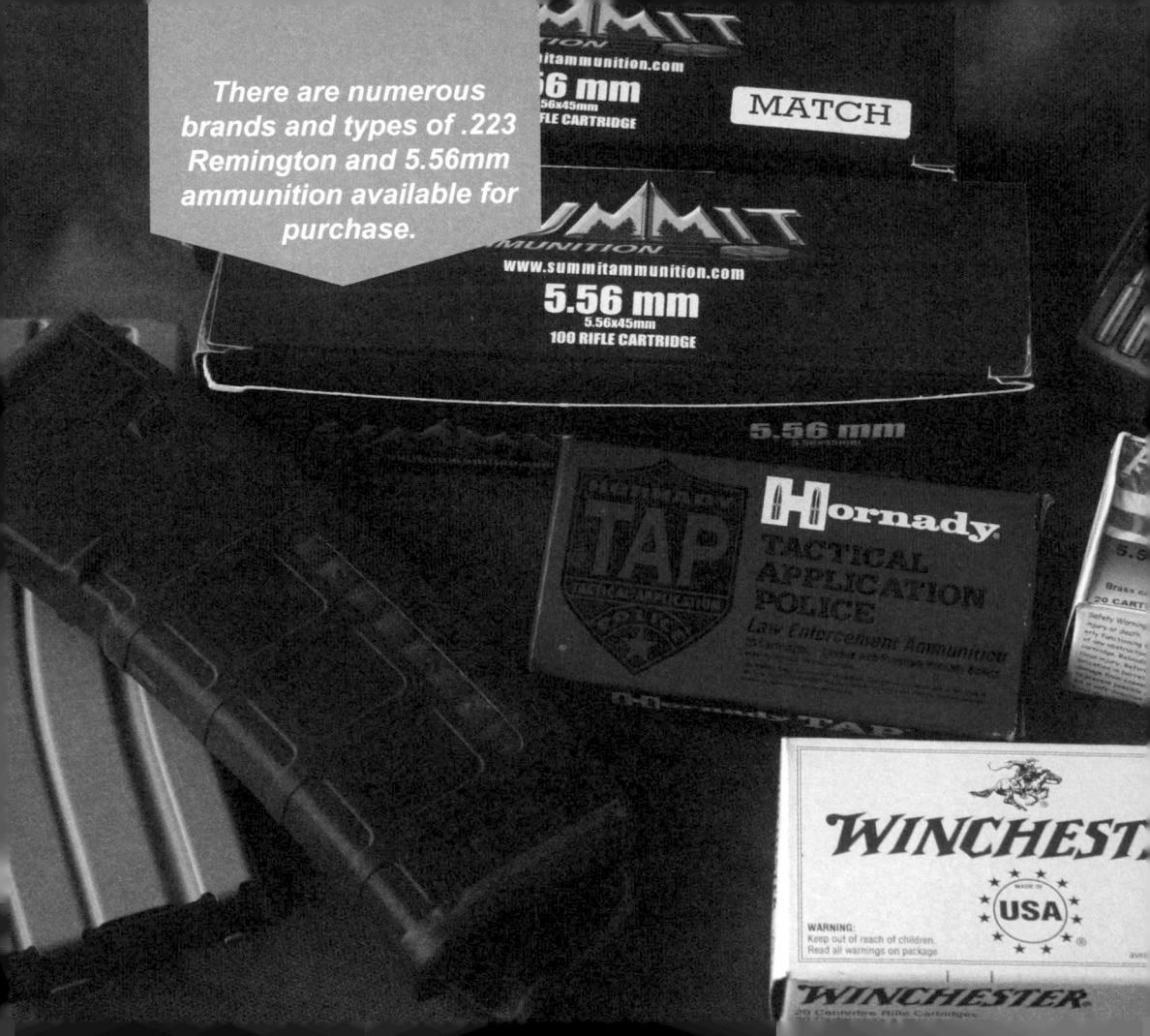

There are numerous brands and types of .223 Remington and 5.56mm ammunition available for purchase.

PRACTICE VS. FIGHTING

If you own a rifle, you should take time to practice with it. With semi-automatic rifles such as the AR or AK, you will likely want to shoot a high volume of ammunition in training and practice. For this, you'll want plenty of full-metal-jacketed ammunition that's manufactured with affordability in mind. Full metal jacket practice ammo—such as that available from American Eagle (Federal Cartridge) and Winchester USA (white box)—tends to be the best bargain. Wolf or Tula ammo, for AK rifles, is popular and affordable.

Separate your practice ammunition from the more expensive and effective controlled expansion ammo. The choice is yours regarding nickel-plated or standard brass cartridges. Nickel-plated cases will withstand the elements better than plain brass, but they are more expensive. Lacquered steel cases, such as those from Hornady or Wolf, are less expensive. However, not all firearms will cycle reliably with steel-cased ammo.

RIFLE AMMUNITION

FIGHTING AMMUNITION

Some folks will say that no rifle below .30 caliber is suited for personal protection. I would say that fifty years ago this might have been the case, but today, such claims hold little weight because modern ammunition has increased the power and energy of even the smallest calibers.

Modern ammunition like .223 Remington or 5.56mm NATO cartridges provide ample energy to stop human predators. The 5.56mm is not an elk or brown bear load, but tens of thousands of dead terrorists and criminals prove the fact that modern 5.56mm ammunition can be quite lethal.

For the .223 Remington or 5.56mm, the heavier weighted projectiles— from 62 grains up to 77 grains—prove more effective when you need to put bullets into something dangerous. The U.S. Army Special Forces

RIFLE AMMUNITION

started using the Mk262 (77g. BTHP) ammunition in M4's in Iraq and Afghanistan roughly a decade ago. This load has a tremendous track record.

The United States Marine Corps is now fielding the Mk318 Mod 0 5.56mm ammunition with a 62 grain controlled expansion projectile. The bullet is rated to travel in excess of 2,900 feet per second when shot from a 14" barreled M4.

As for .30 caliber ammunition, Barnes Bullets produces a number of high quality projectiles. Their TSX and TTSX copper-based projectiles have seen phenomenal success when pitted against animals. Many wild hogs have gone to the great beyond from a single, well-placed TTSX bullet.

RIFLE AMMUNITION

AMMUNITION STORAGE

All ammunition, in any caliber for any firearm, must be stored in a cool, dry environment, since exposure to heat and moisture will reduce its shelf-life. Ammunition cans with a rubber seal (either plastic or the metal US Military surplus versions) are the best for storage. Dropping a moisture absorbing packet into the can is also recommended for extended storage.

The absolute best ammunition to purchase for long-term storage is that which was produced for the United States Military, or produced to "Mil-Spec." Military ammunition is made to be stored long-term. I have personally used military ammunition that was manufactured thirty to forty years before it was unpackaged and fired.

RIFLE AMMUNITION

Surplus Soviet-era ammunition that has been sealed up in "ham can" style can be good for decades. It is dirt cheap and plentiful. My personal experience with this type of ammunition has proven positive. However, it should be noted, this type of ammunition can be very corrosive to your firearm.

There is a company called ZCorr Products that manufactures long term firearm storage bags for the U.S. Military. ZCorr not only makes corrosion resistant resealable bags for guns, but they also make them for parts and ammunition. ZCorr offers ammunition storage bags to line .50 caliber or .30 caliber military ammunition cans. This combination is an excellent choice for storing your loose commercial rounds in steel ammunition cans.

AMERICAN CIVIL WAR, 1861-1865

During the Civil War, the southern states were cut off from supplies, and the Confederacy began to weaken as firearms, powder, and ammunition were severely limited. This not only affected the organized military, but local militias and individual citizens as well.

During almost every historical crisis or emergency, the first thing a sitting government does is forbid the sale of arms and ammunition—or it confiscates them altogether. This has been the historical precedent for hundreds of years, and there is no reason to think it will not continue to be the standard operating procedure.

It is imperative for the citizens to have ample stores of firearms, ammunition, and replacement gun parts before they have the need for them. Once a crisis has been declared, the opportunity to procure such things will be lost.

REAL WORLD SCENARIO: *AMERICAN CIVIL WAR*

EDGED WEAPONS

EDGED WEAPONS

Using edged tools for utility and personal protection is one of the oldest traditions of mankind. Also, it is a tradition that seems to be lost on recent generations. It is a safe assumption that our grandparents and great grandparents carried and used knives, both folding and fixed-blade, on a daily basis.

As society has become more urbanized and "civilized," the knife has become shunned and misunderstood. The reasons are two-fold. First, in an effort to tame the nature of man, many municipalities criminalized the carrying of edged tools. Secondly, as people moved from the countryside to the progressive cultures of the cities, carrying a knife began to seem barbaric and was viewed as an affectation of the common, uneducated, and unrefined man.

The knife is the most basic and useful of all tools. I would encourage you to choose a knife of reputable quality, and then begin carrying it daily. While not the strongest design, the hinged folding knife is popular today because it can be easily carried and concealed at all times. This type of knife is commonly carried daily as a utility tool. It can also serve as a weapon. Many highly regarded manufacturers make tactical folding knives geared toward self-defense. Remember: it's better to have a knife than no weapon at all.

DULL KNIVES ARE USELESS

A dull knife is as ineffective as an unloaded gun. They are also very dangerous as they require more physical exertion to use and increase the chance of accidental injury. People do not treat knives with proper respect. Invariably, people who normally carry dull knives tend to cut themselves with sharp ones because they have grown accustomed to the operation of an unsharpened blade. Sharpened blades cut through

A folding knife is a convenient tool for both utility purposes and self-defense.

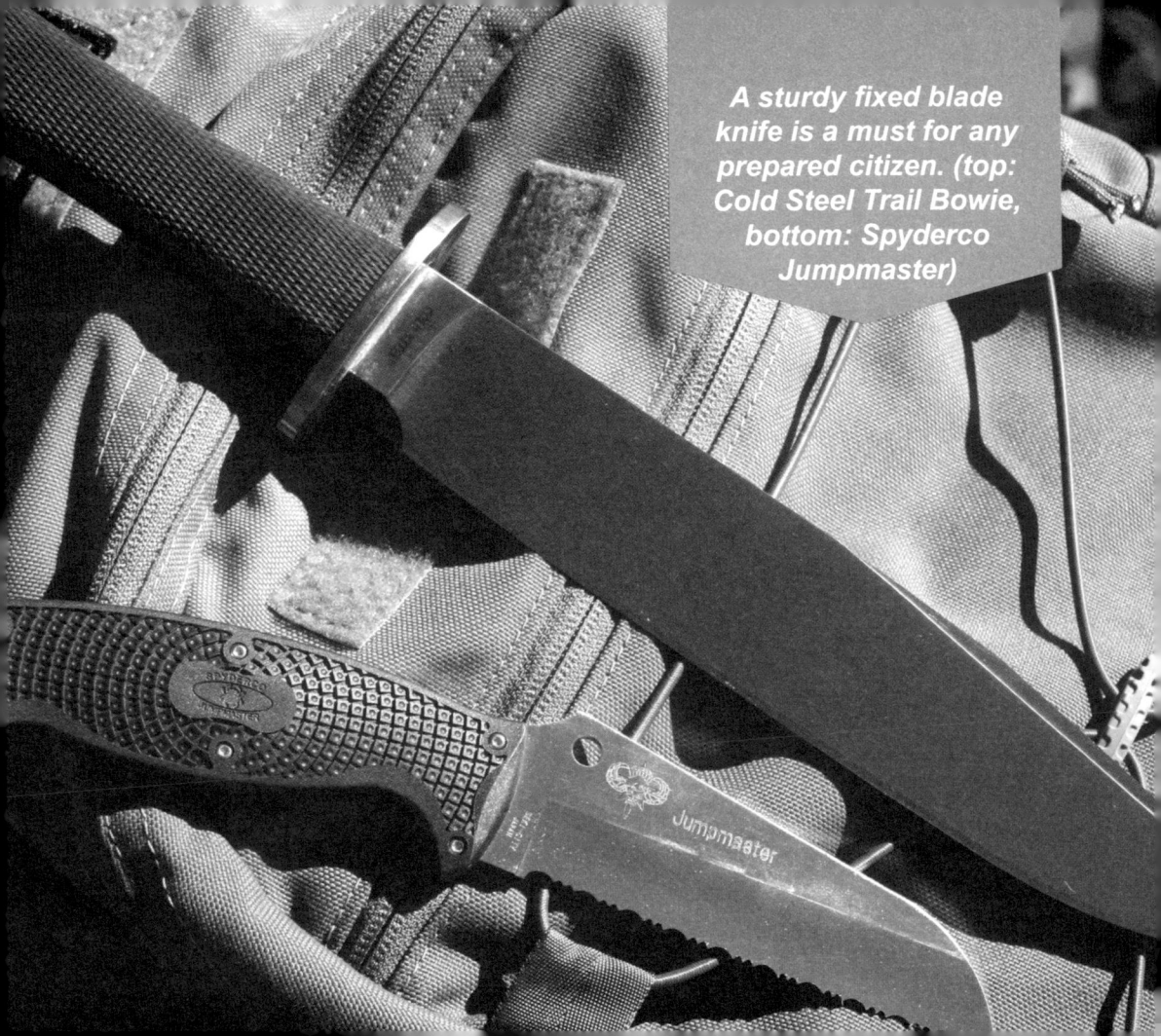

A sturdy fixed blade knife is a must for any prepared citizen. (top: Cold Steel Trail Bowie, bottom: Spyderco Jumpmaster)

materials quickly and easily when compared to those that are dull, and if a user is accustomed to the muscle memory of operating a dull blade, he might get an unpleasant surprise when working with a sharp knife.

Just as people have stopped carrying knives, fathers and grandfathers have stopped teaching their kids and grandkids how to sharpen knives. Every blade will eventually dull if used often. There are a number of resources available online for instruction on honing the edge of a knife. Spyderco, a knife manufacturer, gives fantastic instruction on knife sharpness and how to hone and keep an edge on a blade.

UTILITY AND FIGHTING

Naturally, a knife—whether folding or fixed—will spend the vast majority of its life as a utility tool. However, this does not disqualify its use as a self-defense tool. Before we go one sentence further, you need to get any preconceived images of Hollywood knife fights out of your head. Knife

dueling, where two people circle one another looking for an opportunity to strike, is largely fiction.

Consider any edged weapon to be a force multiplier when you are engaged in a violent struggle. A hand holding a knife can inflict more damage than an empty hand. This is particularly important when a threat is younger, stronger, larger, or greater in number than whoever is being attacked. While this is not a "knife-fighting" book, the purpose of this section is to drive home the idea that you should utilize any available object to protect yourself from any imposing threat.

MACHETES: THE MODERN SWORD

People in third world nations in Central America, Asia, and Africa have been utilizing machetes as combat weapons throughout history. The machete is relatively inexpensive, usually something a peasant can afford. They are much more common than firearms in most areas of the

EDGED WEAPONS

The Cold Steel Gladius machete is unique, as it has dual cutting surfaces with a sharp point.

The Latin Machete (Cold Steel) is the most common, traditional style.

world. Regularly using a machete as a utility tool gives individuals the confidence necessary to effectively turn the machete into a fighting tool.

All well-prepared individuals should have a quality machete on hand. There are innumerable machetes available online and in sporting goods stores. A large percentage of these are worthless junk. A ten-dollar machete is a toy, not a tool.

On a positive note, you can purchase a quality machete from a number of knife companies in the $30 to $40 range. Cold Steel, Gerber, and SOG Knives are just a few companies that produce reliable machetes. Models and styles of machetes vary greatly. The traditional "Latin" machete is likely the most common design. Cold Steel makes a Gladius machete that has a dual edge and a sharp point which most machetes lack.

Whether you are using it to cut away light brush and limbs, prepare kindling, or fend off bad guys, a machete will serve you well in a grid-down situation. I recommend using a machete for light duty yard work, clearing brush when camping, etc., to build familiarity and confidence with it. If you should ever be forced into a situation where you must defend your life with a machete, think of it the same way you would a knife, a force multiplier. The machete offers greater standoff distance and far more reach than even a good fixed-blade knife.

EDGED WEAPONS

EDGED WEAPONS IN HURRICANE KATRINA

When I arrived in post-Katrina New Orleans after the levees failed, I had on my person a Spyderco Pacific SALT folding knife. The blade on the knife was stainless and made of their "H1" rust-free steel.

During the weeks I spent in what seemed like a post-apocalyptic "Big Easy," I used that folding knife for countless chores (including many I never anticipated). The Spyderco folder was perfect for common chores like cutting rope and paracord to construct sun shelters, as well as cutting the shipping bands off of MRE cases for meals.

It was extremely hot and humid with temperatures pushing 90 to 100 degrees each day. Our group was given a cooler full of ice, but the loose cubes almost immediately fused into one giant block. I was able to utilize my Spyderco as an impromptu ice pick.

 REAL WORLD SCENARIO: *HURRICANE KATRINA*

During an afternoon patrol in the French Quarter, we were invited to dine with some federal agents at their outdoor mess hall. The government cooks, via your hard-earned tax dollars, had prepared steak dinners for the agents. I was excited to eat something solid, as I had been living on MREs for two weeks. All that was available was plastic cutlery, which was no good for cutting steak. Fortunately, my Spyderco knife was put to work, and that evening I was a very happy camper.

A good knife will serve you well in a grid-down scenario. Its versatility allows it to be utilized across the board for medical, self-defense, maintenance, and utility purposes, making it an invaluable addition to your arsenal. It would be wise, since quality knives are affordable, to purchase a few of them to be stored in your home, vehicle, go-bag, and bug-out bag.

REAL WORLD SCENARIO: *HURRICANE KATRINA*

Regardless of whether we are speaking in legal or moral terms, not every threatening person or creature that you encounter is going to need to be dealt with through the utilization of deadly force. A well-prepared citizen is someone who prepares for a variety of scenarios surrounding catastrophic situations. Often, this preparation centers on the subject of self-defense. In this section, we will look at situations where non-lethal self-defense tactics might best be used, as well as weapons that can be used to deter individuals rather than kill them.

THE TYPICAL BAD GUY

A potential attacker is not only the typical ski-masked mugger or roving looter. Your attacker could be an unhinged road-rager who believes you cut them off in traffic. You could even be singled-out for a strong-arm robbery by a cab driver, as a friend of mine was recently. Your attacker could be a social bully or a drunk at a restaurant who decides that you offended him in some way. I've even witnessed an irate woman threaten the life of another individual because she claimed they stole her parking

LESS THAN LETHAL

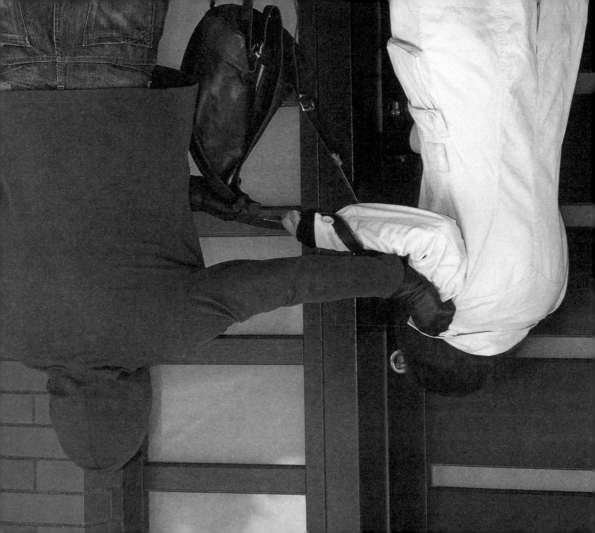

space. All of these characters are potentially dangerous and can pose a threat to your safety and that of your family. Let's take a few moments to consider several tools and methods of dealing with these types of individuals.

OPTIONS: ALTERNATIVE USES OF FORCE

All responsible firearms trainers should advise their students of alternatives to deadly force. I once had a gentleman tell me that he always carried "plenty of firepower" on his person and didn't have time to "worry about things like pepper spray." This mode of thinking is dangerous. Deadly force should always be utilized when it is absolutely necessary. However, if you have no knowledge of or preparation for alternative means, then you only leave yourself with the option to kill. That option isn't always the best.

LESS THAN LETHAL

You cannot justify shooting or even threatening to shoot every person who puts you on edge. Shooting the obnoxious drunk who incessantly hounds you for money will land you in court with a manslaughter or second-degree murder charge. If your life is in jeopardy, you should absolutely do whatever is required to protect yourself. However, despite how it appears in movies, self-defense is not always cut and dry. Real life is much grayer than it is black or white. It is always to your advantage to deescalate or diffuse a situation before deadly force becomes necessary.

PEPPER SPRAY

For nearly two decades, I've been teaching police officers and citizens to properly use Oleoresin Capsicum (pepper spray) as a non-lethal tool for self-defense. Genuine OC products are highly- effective and reasonably priced tools for deterrence.

 **LESS THAN LETHAL**

Genuine OC/Pepper Spray is an excellent non-lethal tool.

A "fighting pen" can be a good alternative for "non-permissive environments."

Permanent injury or scarring is essentially a non-issue when using pepper spray. It causes temporary blindness when sprayed into the eyes and painful burning sensations wherever it falls on the skin. However, after liberal amounts of cold water, the effects of pepper spray will subside.

Pepper spray is designed as a projectile stream which allows you to keep your distance from any threat or target while defending yourself, your family, or your supplies. Pepper spray does not always work instantaneously, as the body chemistry of every individual is different. Some people might be more susceptible to the spray than others and begin to react immediately, while others may require a few more seconds to feel any pain.

Any self-defense product utilized by police that is available to the public for purchase is a great buy. Pepper spray products, such as those made by FOX or Guardian, tend to be much higher in quality than the cheaper products sold at flea markets, swap meets, or a local gas station. Also, be careful when purchasing items online. Many people have been taken advantage of since prepping supplies have become a popular market. Plenty of online stores or individual sellers will sell everything from expired rations and food supplies to shoddily made weaponry. Unless you have researched or know the seller, I would advise you to make your purchases directly from the manufacturer or at brick and mortar stores. When prepping, especially when it comes to self-defense, quality is paramount for survival.

It is important to note, once again, that pepper spray is intended to be utilized as a means of non-lethal force. In a grid-down situation, it would be best used on an unarmed individual who threatens your stock of supplies. For example, a desperate individual who harbors no ill intent may try to covertly steal your supplies to service their own needs. This situation doesn't call for the use of deadly force. However, if your attacker is armed and intends to harm you, then you should use any means necessary to neutralize them.

LESS THAN LETHAL

The C2 Civilian Taser, though expensive, is extremely effective.

MODERN TASERS

The modern Taser should not be confused with a handheld "stun gun." Products from Taser, Inc. are high-tech subject control devices, and they are tremendously effective less-than-lethal weapons. They also protect the user by allowing him to keep distance between himself and a threat. Also, Tasers will immobilize even the biggest of foes once they are zapped by the voltage. In most jurisdictions, Tasers are perfectly legal for citizens to own, carry, and use. However, you should always check your state's laws regarding any weapon.

The drawbacks to Taser units are their expense and single shot capability. While the cartridges are easy to replace, doing so in the middle of an attack is not at all practical. If one or both of the wire-tethered probes miss their mark, then you'll need to move on to another weapon in your arsenal. A stun gun is a viable option, but it requires a user to make direct contact with a target to be effective.

PRACTICAL GEAR

A gun will be one of your primary pieces of equipment should the grid ever go down. It's important to remember that a gun will be your lifeline during that time. It will help defend your home or camp, and it will also be used as your primary hunting tool if you need to secure game for nourishment. If your gun is your lifeline, it makes sense to keep it well maintained. There is a huge cottage industry built around providing gear and accessories to keep your pistols, rifles, and shotguns safe and performing optimally. What we will attempt to do in this section is separate the wheat from the chaff when it comes to practical versus superfluous gadgets for your guns.

HOLSTERS AND SLINGS

Primarily, you will need to have a proper, quality holster to secure your handgun for carry. Long guns will require a durable sling to be carried properly.

PRACTICAL GEAR

The Blackhawk Serpa holster is good for utility and field use, but I don't recommend it for concealed carry.

An inside-the-waistband holster, such as this one from Galco, is a good option for discreet carry.

Many armed citizens put no thought or effort into their choice of a holster. Far too many people put time and effort into researching and buying a pistol or revolver, then, as an afterthought, purchase the cheapest holster they can find. If the gun at your side is there to save your life, I suggest that you invest more than the cost of a burger and fries on a holster. A quality holster will help defend your weapon from dirt, dust, debris, weather, and other potentially negative conditions of your environment. In a grid-down scenario, you may be forced to spend time outside searching for supplies and foraging for sustenance. You will need a holster that can stand up to the elements.

Blackhawk, Bianchi, Blade-Tech, Comp-Tac, Crossbreed, Galco, and Safariland are all companies that produce quality holsters for both concealment and open-carry. These manufacturers offer competitive prices and a range of choices in materials.

A polymer or Kydex holster offers the best resistance to weather and temperature changes. A quality leather holster should be oiled regularly to keep it from becoming brittle or stiff.

PRACTICAL GEAR

Beware of universal holsters. Though they might seem like a good idea, such items are consistently poor in quality and will not secure your gun during strenuous activity. My advice is to purchase a holster that is specifically made for your particular model of handgun.

Think of the sling as a holster for a long gun. Without a sling on your rifle or shotgun you will have to occupy at least one hand holding on to it, or you will constantly be setting the gun down and picking it back up. If you carry for the purpose of self-protection, constantly propping your weapon against a fencepost or a tree is a sure way for the gun to be out of reach if you are approached by a threatening force.

A basic two-point sling that is attached to the front end and the butt-stock is rather universal. For the modern M4, there are single-point attachments with a large loop sling to attach to a single point on the rifle. Both types of slings have their merits and allow you to utilize both of your hands for various tasks while securing your long gun.

Numerous manufacturers produce quality nylon slings at reasonable prices. You should expect to pay somewhere in the neighborhood of

PRACTICAL GEAR

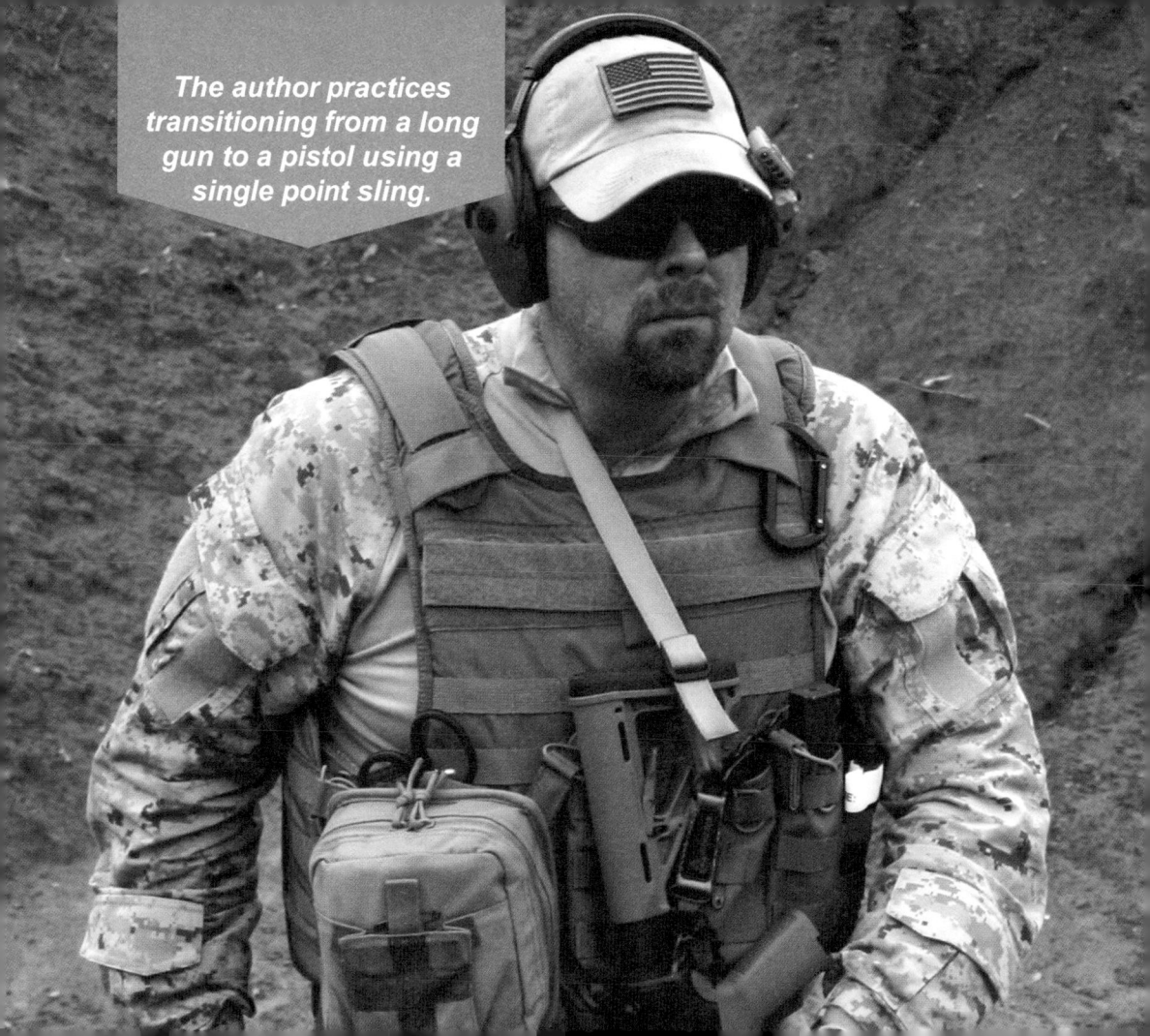

The author practices transitioning from a long gun to a pistol using a single point sling.

A single point sling for a rifle has its merits.

$20-$40 for quality single-point and double-point slings. If your rifle or shotgun is on the heavy side, you might want to spend an extra $5 and purchase a padded sling.

HAND-HELD AND WEAPON-MOUNTED FLASHLIGHTS

The current models of handheld flashlights and tactical lights are being manufactured at the height of modern technology. White LED lights housed in aluminum or high-strength polymer bodies with a tailcap, push-button switch can be used as a non-lethal self-defense tool to administer blunt force.

Any person equipped with a firearm for self-defense should have a white light, whether hand-held or weapon-mounted, handy to help with discernment in dark conditions. It is likely, at some point, during a grid-down situation that you will be caught off guard and possibly left in the dark. It is a good idea to purchase a small, tactical flashlight for everyday carry to accompany your full-bodied, blunt-force flashlight. Keep this smaller flashlight on your person or in your nearby go-bag.

A flashlight has two primary modes when being utilized as a weapon. First, shining your light on a target and commanding them to stop warns them that you are aware of their presence and gives them the ability to disengage you. If an aggressor refuses to heed your warning and continues to be a threat, you can utilize the body of the flashlight as a striking tool.

An individual is responsible for every round he fires. During hours of darkness and diminished light, some form of bright, white light should be used to determine whether a shadow is friend or foe. Could you live with yourself if you nervously fired at a shadow, hit your target, and it turned out to be your spouse or child?

The good news for modern gun purchasers is that gun manufacturers build almost every duty pistol with some type of accessory rail where you can mount a tactical light. In conjunction with this, many flashlight companies are producing tactical lights designed to mount on these rails. A weapon-mounted light allows you to keep both hands on your gun or hold your gun in one hand, leaving the other free to perform other tasks. Also, there are a number of rails and brackets that can be added to the frame of your rifle or shotgun where tactical accessories, including lights, can be mounted.

PRACTICAL GEAR

A bright white light is a must have for every armed citizen.

Grid-Down Tip: If you choose to mount a tactical light onto your firearm, you should go to the range and practice shooting the gun with the light mounted to it. The first time you use your gun/light combination should not be in the middle of a life or death struggle. Also, you will still need some type of non-accessory, handheld light for utility chores to conserve battery life and promote safety.

SUMMARY

This book is in no way meant to be a comprehensive guide on the subject of small arms in terms of being a prepared citizen. Rather, this book was designed to pique your interest and give you some general tips and opinions concerning preparedness for a grid-down situation. Take the principles you have learned in this book and apply them. Begin to research, ask questions, and converse with industry experts so that you might further your understanding and confidence with small arms. I urge you to continue to follow safety rules, train, and prepare.